INSPIRED MOTION

BY

HASHIM RUAN

Forget Everything That You Know

ALL COPYRIGHTS RESERVED TO HASHIM RUAN © 2016

Published in the United Kingdom

motion@sireinspirations.co.uk

ISBN-13: 978-1527203334

No part of this book may be reproduced in any form unless written permission is granted from the author. No electronic copies, storage of any kind may be used or applied to any part of this book/literature without documented or written permission.

Acknowledgements

I would like to express my sincere gratitude and appreciation to the people who have helped me along this journey and making this moment possible.

- I would like to thank the Prince's Trust for their continued support with helping me get this book out to the Market. (Charity Organization registered in England and Wales)

- My mother Ingrid Ruan, for helping with selection and editing of the material. (Senior Banker, Former editor for Sparkle Magazine)

- Ms Tamu Browne for publishing my book online to Amazon market place. (Bachelor of Science (BSc), Management Studies, Past Lecturer in College and Founder of Innovative Education and Training Solutions.

- My Fiancé, Susan Singh for contributing to the design and making sure I complete the book for the intended date.

PREFACE

INSPIRE MOTION. Motion in its rawest form is rough, misdirected, misguided and confused; Motion which is inspired on the other hand, especially internally which no eye can see or fathom, creates a marvelous phenomenon. It is usually the visions we vaguely understand which takes root in our history books. Same goes for nature's wonders, same goes for unexplained mysteries, stories, occurrences etc.

What you do not understand is that life was meant to be a string in the wind, a ball falling from an unknown height, a plane with no landing, a life with meaning unknown. What would be the point of living if we knew all there is to know? 100% brain capacity is already achievable but the key is listening; listening to the part of your brain which can perform the task at hand best.

I have now started observing myself unknowingly by placing cameras around my room because eventually I forget they are there, to see what inspires me most and motivates me to move forward. Then I look at the tapes and take notes and then I will attach it to the part of my brain which was most active. If from this observation I realize, by statistics, that there is a part of my brain not being used I would try and focus on those things but if I redirect by default then I would know what percentage I used most.

That is what method I used to write this book over time, and now I want to share it with the world. I want you to create curiosity in your heart and build it up from the mustard seed it started out to be. Throughout the book, you will have different emotions, views, or judgments and I want you to record them and ask yourself why you felt this way. After you have done this, with those results, apply them to your life's memories and something will happen.

You see the fabric of your reactive emotions, string from your stagnant or passive emotions which harbor in your past memories. To understand and take away as much as you can from this book, you must see it as a method of scrambling and re-organizing your mind so you can think clearly as to what you want to achieve in your life. This method I am calling The Reactive Mind Millennia. May you be inspired from within.

INTRODUCTION

From as far back as WW1 to the silent war of WW3; this is now happening through the industries; a lot of this will start to make sense. There are silent forces which influence our daily actions, such as music and various forms of media. These distractions or diversions and of course various other industries have somehow found a way to fulfill their agenda.

As a result we are still in the problems that we once faced before but in a more civilized and "organized manner". These are, but not limited to;

- Poverty
- Injustice

- Massacres
- Theft
- Witch Craft
- Economic Recession
- Economic Depression
- Human Rights Affairs
- DEATH

Now whether you admit this or not, this is the unfathomable or inevitable truth…but do you know what is most shocking about this truth? **Y0U 1 4LR34DY KN0W**

De Ja Vu is not coincidence or something that may have happened before, it is without a doubt the pinnacle of our deepest memories surfacing at our conscious roots (Present). The Code does not exist…Only does the Truth.

Fear is the greatest illusion of our time and it is the greatest tool of discouragement. When you have fallen many times and when you have fallen so hard where you see recovery as a miracle not a process, when you see no way back to the top, no redemption, and no hope. Just pain…Just suffering…Just heartache…then when you reach the lowest point of your life you realize that it is not worth it. Just take a chance, Just keep trying and trying and trying and trying, you only fail when you stop trying.

"They trade their lives to make money only to spend that money to get their own lives back and living as if they have no life only to die and realize they never lived" – Unknown. There is a universal law that we are aware of but not conscious of, so we live in the same mistakes and era with brand new names and packages.

But then everything changes and you realize that life is not about what you make but what you become and how that affects the people around you and the environment they live in. This life is spontaneous but it is not chance and neither is it stupid. It is beautiful, fearless and undisputedly weird.

Fresh breath…wide open eyes…cellular excitement…pulse throbbing situations are the moments we hold on to but they both hold good or bad emotions, in them whether we like it or not. What are you waiting for? Your neighbor needs you, and so does your invisible being which puts air in your lungs. How much longer my friend?

They continue to make you feel like we are making great movements towards an evolution but we are really moving towards the greatest devastation of human history. Sadly, a world that has given up on their values, and a world which has given up on its inhabitants. Pause and consider. Selah

Hatred? Love? Joy? Change? Action? Choice? No… Only but one is not entirely up to us and that is CH4NG3. Wake up and realize that as one we can and as a statistical population we cannot. Pause and Consider. Selah

When I look at the night's sky I wonder what my mind is pondering. Isn't it interesting that I can actually wonder what my own mind may be twinkling? Super exciting nova thing to consider that and ponder upon the deep of your capabilities and understanding. Alive or dead? And what is death to you and me? Slumber or non-existence? Neither.

CHAPTER 1: A race lost in time

A beautiful symphony like "the moonlight sonata" by Beethoven, on a breezy Sunday afternoon. By the faintest touch on the keyboard, to the softest whisper in the ear of the listener, a message is heard and then what?

Lie with me on this hammock my love and worry not of tomorrow's whim and shambles. Let the wind take you like a leaf to the unexpected wonders of the sky's droplets. Let my arm's warmth be your lullaby and place of refuge in winter's dead night.

What puzzles me most my love is that you stare at me without thought that I too am hurt by your endless tyranny of harmful state, and sad emotion fills my eyes to see you down and under the weather. You are the twinkle of my star, reason for my lung's ability to invite air in day after day.

Do you hear the ocean as it shimmers its way up my spine, moving back and forth endlessly leaving me, leaving you in endless peace of renaissance? I think we need to listen harder as it reminds us of the ocean once used to commute our ancestors. "Lest you forget"

What do you think of at your brightest day or darkest hour? I can let you into my heart for a brief moment on this, because this relates to us all as we still do not understand why we were placed on this planet at this given time and in this given space we call the universe.

I have something to tell you…L12T3N C4R3FULLY. Be Quiet, 'the piano starts to play' again silent your mind, and open your heart. We are the same, we suffer the same fate, you are no different than me but the choices you make are. Look at your eyes aren't they beautiful, look at them throb with excitement and wonder.

Fret not my neighbor rather fear not you are not alone. Whether they want to believe you or not you have something that they are afraid of, something that you will use one day and that is your mind. The sad thing is that some of you use it when your temple can no longer serve you or those around you whether alive or dead.

The bliss of life's failures is that you can decide to let them get you down or you can decide to continue forging forward. Take a moment and think of the day you were born, was that coincidence or was that fate? The interesting thing about uncertainty is that the answer is simply in a scramble not lost or unreachable.

People tend to think that they understand you and what you are trying to say or what you are going through but you know what I am here to tell you? I don't even understand myself, (dramatic pause) and I won't sit here and pretend that I know you either. But have we ever wondered that maybe there is nothing wrong with not understanding something?

Sometimes it is okay not to understand and not to comprehend, it is one of the greatest wonders of life. It sparks the greatest force known to mankind and that is curiosity. Curiosity makes no judgment and is genuinely passionate about its unknown prey.

Pause and Consider. Selah

IT IS Ok to be YOU. Stop trying to be someone you are not. Break the status quo.
—Hashim Ruan

I have grown weary of trying to explain myself to others at the age of 21 but by the age of 38 I think I will become metal after being tempered and heated until it becomes the desired product. By then it will be too late my love. This is my greatest fear, so I seek to be tempered and heated now so that I may shine well before God and before Men.

Won't you agree that we all have many questions that are unanswered? Well there is a reason why answers take so long to come about and that is because of nation separation and statistical population. We would rather win wars and have national pride than realize that there are no borders, there are no waters but rather water, there are no skies but rather there is a sky.

What is this non sense about being American and Caribbean and Middle Eastern or European and Asian? We are but one thing and that is human. Who cares about who was the first civilization? Get over yourselves we have one life, one world, one chance to make it right with each other. When am gone an apology won't mean a thing.

Only the very living God cares about dead apologies, but the guy or girl that died will not hear it. Be kind for crying out loud. Get over the fact that you or your neighbor suffered and just help each other. I am getting really confused about why we are here not because of anything God did or God said but because we continue to make the same mistakes and wonder why the 1% billionaire continue to win the game.

Just how you can be committed to reading a book just before your own exam is committed to helping a kid without something to receive in the first place; Stop being so selfish. How can you sleep well at night knowing that your neighbor still suffers for the morrow?

Do you hear that? It is your God forsaken conscience biting your ear to do something about what you are hearing. The conscience is like an invisible programmed software that only works when action is needed so if yours is not working it can only mean one out of two things. You are either already doing something about it or you are afraid to do something about it. Other than that you are probably dead.

Let me firstly say I am sorry for one thing after I said all that, and that is that I too have made these mistakes. That is what I am trying to tell you. No book that has ever been written, no speech that has ever been given, is being done by anyone who is different from you and me. But that is the whole point of this narration we are having together. That you become aware that we must not only accept our wrong doings but everyone else's.

When that happens we will focus more on the solutions than the problems we face as a human race. Whether it is sickness or pain, failure, or the next big idea…we can all do it together but if we think that we are here to be better than the other we will always have strife.

By now <u>you</u> are probably passing judgments and assuming into the matter of who is the narrator or author of this book. <u>You</u> should stop and ask <u>your</u>self if that is the question. The author of this book and forever will be <u>YOU</u>. Yes <u>you</u> because author here means interpreter and mental scripter. Even though <u>you</u> are reading my words, <u>you</u> are writing <u>your</u> own *version in <u>you</u>r head. Whether consciously or subconsciously and <u>you</u> need to stop it! Passing judgments I mean.*

Now while I was speaking just now you were observing the fact that I underlined each you in that paragraph. If that is true, if you haven't done it already I want you to count the number of times it was used and pause and consider. Selah

Wow is it morning already? Let's get some sleep before your head explode. Or would you rather read on? OK…fine let's continue. So my next question would be is…Who are you? And why are you reading this book?

Most of you would say things like this; I was curious to see the writer's work, I have nothing else better to do and those of you who love reading would say you love reading. But how many of you can say you have read this book to better yourself…not materialistically but your very mind.

It is no secret that the mind is your greatest resource for memory and skill logging. But also the greatest tool that basically pulsates the reality of opportunity in the most wildly imaginative sense of the word, dreams!!

I have a story to share with you and it is of my pasts past where I was given the opportunity to be whatever I want to be in life and I had two choices. Be main stream or be me. Now this was the most confusing riddle of my life because there is such a thin line between the two, you can often find yourself becoming main stream by also being YOU.

So I realized in order to find that balance I had to be me in a spontaneous and organized manner where I never lose sight of what I wanted in life while being creative on a day to day basis so I don't become habitual or stuck.

Today is also a combination of now and tomorrow because time never stops so take a moment and view it from this angle. Time never stops right? So tomorrow is not sitting on a bench waiting, it is actual running with the baton and if you don't do what you have to do to catch that next runner, you will lose the race. But just as importantly so will those who are running the race with you.

Which means success keeps going just like time? If time doesn't stop why should you? So whatever it is you want to achieve, you have to find a way to keep the train moving even when you are sleeping. So here's a hint, there are different time zones in the world so get a multinational team. No one can stay awake for 24 hours.

So you have at least 8 hours that you need for sleep right. Start looking for someone who can work when you are sleeping but obviously he or she has to work in a different time zone than you. Now pause and consider. Selah

OK let's not lose focus here. I have something to share with you now that may challenge everything that you know and believe in. I am here for you so do not ever lose hope. If no one else cares, I care. Listen carefully…What you have is not what you are. What you have is what you do. And what you are is how you think.

If someone tells you that you are small minded and you believe them then it is true and you believe that about yourself. If someone says you can't do something and you believe them then you never had a motive or passionate reason. There is a difference between a reason and a passionate reason. A reason is a predictive or conclusion cause of one's actions. A passionate reason is a heartfelt purpose for ones actions despite obstruction.

So I just gave you two important tools in life for success whether on the fast track or slow track life train. Yes that's right this book is not just for those who are directionless but for those who already have direction but that direction hasn't necessarily given them the happiness and fulfillment they were looking for. Like Chris Brown who made that confession about worshipping the wrong person all these years.

Money is not accumulated through hard work but rather creative and problematic thinking. If you can't realize your own problems how can you solve them? And how can you make money if you don't appear to be different from the person behind you, beside you or around you? The key to making money is to first recognize what problem you are trying to solve and how you will beat your greatest competition.

Your greatest competition is yourself my friend. If you cannot beat that competition or at least make peace with it, you cannot strive in business or even in your regular day to day life. Competition here means your own negative voice and your own self inflicting thoughts or habits. Now overcoming this enemy is not an easy game to win.

You have to accept two things or better yet remember two things. Never get angry with this enemy and never take on more than you can chew because defeat is much easier. This enemy knows more about you than your conscious self. You may even be shocked at some of the things you find out.

The enemy is your deepest desires and wildest dreams. It is your deepest fear and brightest evil. This is your to be or not to be. This is the ultimate graduation in life. This is the answer to peace and the answer to happiness. Finding yourself and what was lost over time is what is important. You see, you don't want to find yourself because you are afraid of what you find.

You need to grow up and realize you have nothing to lose. Stop comparing about what your friend has in comparison to you. You came into this life with nothing so what do you have to lose really? Nothing! Get up, get out and do something for your dream! God said it is more profitable to gain your soul than gain the world so focus on making soul filled achievements.

So what if you fail? God said I AM God Almighty and He made you in his image and likeness. You are flesh but empowered by God, imbued with grace and power and all you believe him for. Wake up and remember. Can't Stop, Won't Stop!

Good morning I trust you had a good night's rest because I definitely needed a break from writing. How are you? Great to hear you are doing well. Now that you have graduated from the first question, it is now time for my next question, "where do you see yourself in the next 5 years?" How do you plan on getting there? And why do you want to be at that place in your life?

Now I know you are probably going to have some trouble actually responding to this question because we all do. These are some heavy questions that bear a lot of consequences and outcomes. I do know that some of you on your first try will have responses like "Married, Have a house, Have a car, and about three kids". Well before you say that, please don't. Those are goals and that has nothing to do with where you see <u>you</u>rself in 5 years.

So you are probably confused at this point and being confused is good because it means you are thinking and you actually are curious to find out what it is am talking about. Now in that sentence if you look closely at what is being said. "WHERE" suggests a destination but destination is not an ending but rather a place of reevaluation for the next step forward. "DO" also suggests that it takes persistent action to move from year 'now' to year 'later'. "YOU" means only you can do it and no one is going to get up every day and do it for you. "SEE" means you need to also keep your eyes open for what is true and what is not and stay true to your vision. "YOURSELF" means don't be afraid to be you and look in the mirror and be the reason for your drive, if you aren't passionate about your well-being or success you won't get anywhere.

"5 years" means you need to be a person of time and always set goals one day at a time. Years are made of 365 days not 365 hours. Pace yourself and don't take on too much. Lastly, how and why are you doing or trying to do what you are on the path towards. So below now would be 5 things to consider for each day and each year until that mark is reached.

- *Consider your environment and the people around you because the "Where" in the present will determine the "where" in the next five years.*
- *Look at your actions daily and ask yourself this, "Do they match what I want to succeed?*
- *Your heart beats all the time to keep you alive are you keeping the beat alive for your dreams?*
- *Vision is not blind to bad it sees both good and evil.*
- *Self Acceptance is the first step to moving anywhere in life*

So you know what's next? The pinnacle or peak of your life is what is next. Pause and consider. Selah

CHAPTER 2: Lost years at your grasp…

The phrase above gives you a sense of recovery or rejuvenation. Now the pinnacle or peak of one's life is not just the greatest time of your life in a positive way but it can also refer to the highest form of suffering you have ever endured which can then produce something great in your life.

When someone says you have reached your peak this doesn't necessarily mean your best moment or time but your most important time of revelation and reward. So this brings us to our next graduation ceremony where I will not ask you a question but reveal some truth to you that may or may not change your life.

In 1926 not too far from when I was born, a genius in his unorthodox and opened mind predicted world news, cell phone and great communication networks, but you know he also forecasted and foresaw the future of our human destination of where we would be in our thinking and that technology will make us lazy.

Shortly After that an extraordinary man rose up in 1976 and brought out a revolutionary line of cell phone that has changed the face of communication and mobile units forever. Now this man died early, not too long after his legacy was already built but he always restricted his children from using the very invention he created.

Why you ask? Because he understood the morale and purpose of technology but he also realized that he created a 21st Century technology which is for a people who are not necessarily informed of the correct uses. So initially he started teaching people how to use them the right way but some where the vision got lost somewhere in between there.

In 2004 another genius came along and created a communication network that has allowed us to live close to our families without being close to each other. Connecting with family and friends thousands of miles away but the difference was that this network was "free". But was it really? I think in reality privacy, security and anti-socialism was the cost.

So what's my point here? When you reach to the top of a mountain, can you tell me what's on the other side or what's in the view? The answer is another path or another peak to climb. Now nature has an odd way of teaching us about our everyday lives but it speaks nothing but the truth.

The point here is that there is not just a peak or a pinnacle. There are many peaks and many pinnacles which mean the reason why we always fail or always stop striving is because we think that when we get that big cheque or big house that this is the end. Well my friend this is really just the beginning of your real purpose.

Nikola Tesla, Steve Jobs, And Mark Zuckerberg all appear to have one thing in common and that is believing that after they have made something great and it makes them rich then that is it or because it was so hard to get the first dream accomplished there is no use in trying to do something else. So they build on that one accomplishment. The solution to that problem is to change how you view things. Facebook was not an accomplishment for Mark it was a step closer to what we want to achieve as a race.

So I think the role of every visionary and entrepreneur is to pass the baton and stop trying to create riches to get on the bill board of world's richest or smartest kid but rather start looking for that next step by being open and committed to find that next person. We are all a part of one body, each cell cannot carry out every function but in fact each cell has their role to carryout to ensure the body progresses from infant to baby to adolescence to adult to death.

Good morning again guys I had to seriously get some rest because it was taking a toll on my health there. But I am back and feeling refreshed. So how are you? And where were we? Ahh yes that's right your pinnacle so am hoping by now this book has made a tremendous change in your life. I'm assuming that it has, because you would have hopefully learned some truths that some people are still searching for.

Now this brings us to our runner up graduation session. This is about the statement we all have made so famous "Life is so unfair and life is so hard". Well I am here to enlighten you that it is the biggest lie you can tell yourself or anyone for that matter because life is pretty simple and pretty easy. Living is hard, when you bust a move, when you work hard, when you go towards your dreams that is when you can utter the words "Living is hard but life is easy".

What you have to remember is that life is seen through the involuntary actions of the heart or of your lungs or even of your mind but as soon as you choose to speed things up or take in more air than you need, that's when things start to switch up. My son and my daughter (youths) you have to remember something, this life was not designed to be steered alone or on your own strength. You have to start thinking deeper and realize this life is bigger than you but you can be bigger than life if you just start living.

Get up off the couch and look yourself in the mirror and tell yourself, "No more will I ever take the back seat!" "No more will I say okay!" As a matter of fact it is not okay, it never is okay to settle for something you never asked for or worked for. It is never okay to be degraded or told that you are not good enough.

Open your eyes and see that you have the power in your mind to do anything you want. Water and electricity may not be free but ideas are! So get quiet and shut out the world because your day starts today my friend. Not someday but today, never have I seen someday on a calendar but I sure have seen Monday and all the days of the week.

Stop being a coward and face your fears! Listen to that voice that says you won't ever get pass high school and use that as ammunition for the next battle of your life. Okay I'll calm down now because I may say things that aren't appropriate for some readers so I'll calm down.

So here's my next question are you making a living or are you designing a life? Pause and consider. Selah

CHAPTER 3: Your Grand design

The author of your walk with me... Feel free to make appropriate your attire and wits. Spare me the empty vile of your bloody folly and simply move with your neurons. I love what you have done with your tightly fitted follicles, quite invigorating I might add. Freshly baked in the oven of life... Hush those heavy eyes fret not to open them as the bright force is too much to bear.

You are no vile creature as the world tries to paint you to be, you are winged loved one of Elohim. Surely you think me for a fool if you make me to believe the lies of sheep. Lovely bones of innocence speak with your gestures, not your flattery beauty. Listen carefully with the wind in your sacks and the sparkle in your form. I Love You. Not a worry in the world my fragile one, only wonder what comes next in your greatest journey.

Who says heaven cannot be found earlier rather than later. You just lay down there in your softest and most inexplicable existence, harming no one or nothing. What are your plans love, are they ones of anguish or torment or those of roses in a river, joy and growth? I think the latter but greater is my desire to find your design within your movement. Rest your limbs littlest wolf for what is ahead is greater than any hunger for thy mother's suckling.

Build a life/business that will even be needed in a crisis or recession. There is no question that with how the world is going at the moment, that your business or more importantly, your life, has to be ready for even the worse conditions. Make sure it is built on values, make sure it allows you to express yourself, and make sure each time you think of why you are doing it, it makes you smile.

Build worth beyond the money you have in your bank account, always have a place of retreat and the best part is that it can be in your very mind. Actually, my retreat is my baby boy or girl. Inspire, do not try to change because change is an inevitable and abrupt force which cannot be stopped and often with good intentions but seen as something bad in most cases.

Inspire because it is sweet, soft and often lasts forever. Live for love not for yourself or others because love increases and can never fail. Love increases happiness, Love increases wealth, Love improves health. Love is unbeatable. Well as for yourself and others I think that is self explanatory. A story never told is lost forever so speak with your diaphragm not with your chest and let free.

The first person to be honest with is yourself, because within you is an eternal record of things you say and if it is a lie then eventually you will become that lie. Mistakes are lies trying to find the truth because intuition tells you what to do but yet you do the opposite and expect everything to be okay. No.

Mistakes are actually a way of the universe saying well done but you should have done it the other way instead nevertheless get up and move on. Self pity is poison not edification; please do not confuse it for the latter. Your explicit, unapologetic, untainted, graceful design; Formed and brewed by your essence of thought and marrow, dense and thickened by life's digestion and channels be still.

What is death to you really? At most points in my life I feared death. I would rather die fighting a battle with an enemy I see than with one I cannot. The latter is all but sudden and often comes without fair warning or mercy. A battle with one you can see is purely up to you, for if you fail surely you can get back up, but if you win you will never have to return.

You see the war is never external but internal, a never ending roller coaster of woes and heights, sights and kites, meadows or streams. Like the beating in my chest and the swaying on my neck and not short of the spark in my vein. This is the essence of my being and beyond this are my wildest imagination which extends beyond the stars with man's ignorant devices and fables. Each day I crumble and rise again from the ashes.

So let's talk about your plans now, I will go out on a limb here and say you are young and probably trying to figure things out in your own life or without any one's help. Well we all know in this day and age nothing is ever accomplished on one's own whits whether inspired or transpired. Conspire not against your brethren because he is not about your demise but only curious of your progress.

To be human is to be kind. That is why when you look upon an animal, they call it in humane. Strive not strife, embrace do not defend; more often than not we try to change the natural order. Even in our own food supply –whispers- we are mad too! In a good way, rather than not because in our subconscious over active minds, we try to fix things that are already perfectly imperfect. I do not think we know better because in a world so broken we often forget the difference between the two.

Granted, that this will be one of the coldest winters for environmental reasons but at least there is a spring to look forward to! Thing about life is, we were granted it, but it is a grant that comes with conditions. Usually grants are free money with conditions either way, for example, you have to go to a certain school, or you have to own a certain type of business.

Why do we think life is any different? Life is a grant given before the conditions, but the conditions were attached in the folder most of us failed to read. Some conditions of life we fulfill subconsciously, like breathing. If you want to achieve anything however, the conditions can change in a moment's notice, so what should we do you ask? We should accept them as fast as we accept conditions when downloading apps-- no we should ask and seek guidance in any shape or form we know best. Reason behind it being, that when we bypass conditions we run into problems.

A simple concept we fail to carry out regularly and expect amazing results. We forget and fail to realize that hard work is the name of any target. That attitude of not going the extra mile because no one cares or no one will pay you for is a loser's mind set. If you aren't willing to be the hardest worker in the room and sacrifice your social time, party time or sleep time; most likely what you will end up with is a mediocre life.

This is no time to be mediocre-- as a matter of fact; there was never a time my friends. Hard work has no short cut and neither does success. When you become successful it doesn't end there. The Rock is now the highest paid actor in the world. Does that mean he wasn't successful before? Absolutely not! He just knew that to keep up with the game, he had to step up his level of grinding. Study it and be blessed!

Time is such an elusive, evasive, amazing thing-- Time is easily lost but can never be regained. Money is easy to gain and is easily lost; love is easily lost and hard to gain. The beautiful truth is though, that love is easily given but not easily received, money is easily received but not easily given. Time however remains the same, there is a reason why no matter what you do in life time can never be regained; the reason is because life is a gift, a gift as you know cannot be given twice, so you must enjoy it and savor it while you can. The answers to life as we are told for our math's exam are all on the paper we are taking. Read between the lines of your experiences and highlight the good memories. You see-- life is not singular, it is a plural collage of stories, and everyone has their own copy of a book. Life is written and Life is read but you choose what is published and what is lost forever.

MAY YOU BE INSPIRED FROM WITHIN

INSPIRED MOTION

www.ingramcontent.com/pod-product-compliance
Lightning Source LLC
Chambersburg PA
CBHW041756040426
42446CB00001B/57